LES MURRAY

Waiting for the Past

CARCANET

First published in Great Britain in 2015 by
Carcanet Press Limited
Alliance House
Cross Street
Manchester
M2 7AQ

www.carcanet.co.uk

First published in Australia in 2015 by Black Inc.,
an imprint of Schwartz Media Pty Ltd,
Level 5, 289 Flinders Lane, Melbourne, Victoria 3000 Australia

We welcome your comments on our publications
Write to us at info@carcanet.co.uk

A CIP catalogue record for this book is available from the British Library

ISBN 978 1 784101 16 9

The publisher acknowledges financial assistance from Arts Council England

Typeset by XL Publishing Services, Exmouth
Printed and bound in England by SRP Ltd, Exeter

Waiting for the Past

Les Murray was born in 1938 and grew up on a dairy farm at Bunyah on the north coast of New South Wales. He studied at Sydney University and later worked as a translator at the Australian National University and as an officer in the Prime Minister's Department. Since 1971 he has made literature his full-time career, publishing over 30 books and receiving numerous awards, including the T.S. Eliot Prize, the Petrarch Prize, the Mondello Prize, and The Queen's Gold Medal for Poetry.

Contents

To the glory of God

The Black Beaches

Yellow rimming the ocean
is mountains washing back
but lagoons in cleared land often
show beaches of velvet black

peat of grass and great trees
that were wood-fired towers
then mines of stary coals
fuming deep in dragon-holes.

This morning's frost dunes
afloat on knee-sprung pasture
were gone in a sugar lick
leaving strawed moisture

but that was early
and a change took back the sun
hiding it in regrowth forest.
Coal formed all afternoon.

Inspecting the Rivermouth

Drove up to Hahndorf:
boiled lamb hock, great scoff!
Lamplit rain incessant.

Next morning to the Murray mouth,
reed-wrapped bottlings of view
grigio and verdelho.

Saw careers from the climbing bridge,
the steel houses it threw
all over Hindmarsh Island,

the barrages de richesse,
film culture, horseradish farms,
steamboats kneading heron-blue

lake, the river full again.
Upstream, the iron cattle bridges.
So. Then a thousand miles

home across green lawn.

The Canonisation

Rome, 17 October 2010

Mary MacKillop, born 1842,
what are the clergy giving you
on my birthday, Mother Mary?

Sainthood? So long after God did?
Independence? But you're your own Scot.
The job of Australian icon?

Well yes. Black flies in the buggy.
Bush pianos. The cheek-sawing wimple
in summer: you did do local penance.

Your vow to "educate poor children" –
might you now say "to heal
the education of poor children?"

Who says a woman can't rise
in the Church? Mother Mary,
awake in Heaven, pray for us.

High Rise

Fawn high rise of Beijing
with wristwatch-shaped
air conditioners on each window

and burglar bars to the tenth
level in each new city,
white-belted cylinders of dwelling

around every Hong Kong bay –
Latest theory is, the billions
will slow their overbreeding

only when consuming in the sky.
Balconious kung fu of Shanghai.
A nineteenth floor lover

heroic among consumer goods
slips off the heights of desire
down the going-home high wire –

above all the only children.

Nuclear Family Bees

Little native-bee hives
clotted all up the trunk
of a big tree by the river.

Not pumped from a common womb
this world of honey-flies
is a vertical black suburb

of glued-on prism cells.
Hunters stopping by
would toe-walk up,

scab off single wax houses
and suck them out, as each
smallholder couple hovered

remonstrating in the air
with their life to rebuild,
new eggs, new sugarbag,

gold skinfulls of water.

When Two Percent Were Students

Gorgeous expansion of life
all day at the university,
then home to be late for meals,
an impractical, unwanted boarder.

When rush hours were so tough
a heart attack might get stepped over
you looked up from the long footpaths
to partings in the houses' iron hair.

Hosts of Depression-time and wartime
hated their failure, which was you.
Widows with no facelift of joy
spat their irons. Shamed by bookishness

you puzzled their downcast sons
who thought you might be a poofter,
so you'd hitchhike home to run wild
again where cows made vaccine

and ancient cows discovered aspirin,
up home, where your father and you
still wore pink from the housework
you taught each other years before –

and those were the years when farm wives
drove to the coast with milk hands
to gut fish, because government no longer
trusted poor voters on poor lands.

I Wrote a Little Haiku

I wrote a little haiku
titled *The Springfields*:

Lead drips out of
a burning farm rail.
Their Civil War.

Critics didn't like it,
said it was obscure –

The title was the rifle
both American sides bore,
lead was its heavy bullet
the Minié, which tore

often wet with blood and sera
into the farmyard timbers
and forests of that era,
wood that, burnt even now,

might still re-melt and pour
out runs of silvery ichor
the size of wasted semen
it had annulled before.

Dynamic Rest

Six little terns
feet gripping sand
on a windy beach

six more just above
white with opened wings
busy exchange of feet

reaching down lifting off
terns rising up through terns
all quivering parallel

drift ahead and settle
bracing their eyes
against the brunt of wind

Foyles Bookshop
Unit 22, Lower Concourse
Waterloo Station, London SE1 8SW
Tel: 0203 206 2680
email orders@foyles.co.uk
www.foyles.co.uk
VAT Reg: GB 238 7687 10

12-10-15 17:52   SALE 25   13760
You were served by: DanielLWC

PRODUCT	QTY	VAT
WAITING FOR THE PAST		
9781784101169	1	9.99 Z
Zero Rate	9.99	9.99
TOTAL	1	9.99
VAT		0.00
CASH		20.00
TOTAL TENDERED		20.00
CHANGE		10.01

West Coast Township

Cervantes. This one-strum pueblo
seen beyond acorn banksia
along a Benedictine surf –
never the Oz end of a cable, though.

How Spanish was the Indian Ocean?

Well, not. Except for basque Sebastian
de Elcano, centuries off Perth:
*Of mankind, only we in my ship shall
have made a full circuit of Earth…*

even as scurvy kept their ebb low.

Money and the Flying Horses

Intriguing, the oaten seethe
of thoroughbred horses in single stalls
across a twilit cabin.

Intimate, under the engines' gale,
a stamped hoof, a loose-lip sigh,
like dawn sounds at track work.

Pilots wearing the bat wings
of intercontinental night cargo
come out singly, to chat with or warn

the company vet at his manifests:
four to Dubai, ten from Shannon,
Singapore, sixteen, sweating their nap.

They breed in person, by our laws:
halter-snibbed horses radiating over the world.
Under half-human names, they run in person.

We dress for them, in turn. Our officer class
fought both of its world wars in riding tog:
Luftwaffe and Wehrmacht in haunched jodhpur pants.

Stumbling turbulence, and the animals
skid, swivelling their large eyes
but iron-fisted rear-outs calmed by revolver shot

are a rarity now, six miles above
the eventing cravat, the desert hawking dunes.
Handlers move among the unroofed stalls.

They're settling down, Hank:
easy to tell, with stallions;
they must be the nudest creatures alive –

Tomorrow, having flown from money to money
this consignment will be trucked and rested
then, on cobble, new hands will assume the familiar

cripple-kneed buttock-up seat
of eighteenth-century grooms
still used by jockeys.

Sun Taiko

Across the river
outside of towns
farm machinery for sale
in wire compounds

Pumpkin to all of it
are rainwater tanks
plastic, mostly round
edge on, ribby flanks
a few Roman IIIs

most in cool Kiwi tones
sage, battleship, dun
two thousand litres, ten
each with a rimmed
O hole for sound

Persistence of the Reformation

Seen from the high cutting
the sky drifts white cotton
over dance-floors of water
either side the shady creek
that trickles down country
lagoons gummed with water fern

saucepans of wet money
brass polyester gold
couch grass black in swamp
lily dams backed up gullies
and parallel in paspalum
old tillages that fed barns

no one grows patch-crops now
slow-walking black cattle
circle up off cleared flats
past pastel new brick houses
and higher charcoal-barreled
hills are fields of a war

four hundred years of ship-spread
jihad at first called
the Thirty Years War
buff coats and ships' cannon
the Christian civil war
of worldwide estrangement

freemasons, side massacres
the nun-harem, Old Red Socks
wives "turning" for husbands
those forbidden their loves
bitter chews of an old plug
from Ireland and Britain

while mutual help and space
and breach of cliché and face
here civilized the boundary fences
bigot slurs jostled tempers
right up into the dairy age
new killings back

in cold lanes of the Boyne
shamed it all on the news
among Christmas homecomings
the local dead
still mostly lie in ranks
assigned them by denomination
though belief may say Ask Mum
and unpreached help
has long been the message.

Child Logic

The smallest girl
in the wild kid's gang
submitted her finger
to his tomahawk idea –

It hurt bad, dropping off.
He knew he'd gone too far
and ran, herding the others.
Later on, he'd maim her brother.

She stayed in the bush
till sundown, wrote
in blood on the logs, and
gripped her gapped hand, afraid

what her family would say
to waste of a finger.
Carelessness. Mad kids.
She had done wrong some way.

Floodtime Night Shelter

No mattress for the last levee shoveller,
estates of damp clothing rather
and groceries and crises on the netball
squeak floor, within sidelong of the river.
Roped curtain to let underpants be shed,
mulch of blankets half dry, and how
to keep four cushions in line
underback, with clay and shift-off
as of islands in continental drift-off.
Discreet knees up for sex or
to check the infiltering depth of water
far off houses colliding in main stream.
These were many nights of that year.

Powder of Light

Hunched in the farm ute
tarpaulin against wind
the moon chasing treetops
as it yellows into night
us, going to the pictures
by the State forest way
my mate's brother driving

we are at the age
that has since slipped
down toward toddlers
for whom adults and dreams
mostly have no names yet.
What wagged on screen then
made from powder of light

were people in music
who did and said dressy
stuff in English or American
kissed slow with faces crossed
flicked small-to-big
in an instant, then
were back in Australia

we believed it was Australia –
then our driver who never
attended films would surface
from courting and collect us
there way before TV.
And people, some holding
phones like face cards, still ask

good movie? Who was in it?
I smile and say Actors
but rarely now add
hired out of the air.

The Backroad Collections

Verandah shops with history
up roads like dry-gully bends
proffer gouts of laundered colour
out into their gala weekends,

recycled fashion displayed
under bullnose eaves, down corridors,
cerise, magenta, nubbled teal,
lilac overalls that were a steal,

yellow bordure and buttony rib,
pouched swimsuits, cretonne ad lib
in front of blush-crimson sleeves.
Craft collectors carry off sheaves,

tie dye, mai tai, taupe lingeries –
and cattle who haven't yet entered
any building wander, contented,
munching under their last trees

till a blowsy gold-ginger horizon
stacked up out of the day's talk
glorifies and buries the sun.
A nude moon burns the newsprint version.

Tap Dogs Music

Ponderous cauldrons
roaring with air
white gold slopping over
smoke fallout everywhere

Open the tap-hole
steel light is blind
intense as a searchlight
infinitely confined

The scorched hook-steerers
down in the spatter
spend crib times heel-and-toeing
a new ferrous patter

on sheets of cooled plate
since these works will soon close
and spangling metal
will set in black floes.

English as a Second Language

A coffee cart was travelling down the mountain,
in the yellow shape of an ice-cream coupe it travelled,
a cappuccino on wheels.
                                    And we followed, speaking
of this American teenager who was sent
to remedial English, since he spoke more Tagalog.
An American in remedial!
His military parents had been deep
in the Asian preoccupation. When he came back
on a visit, it was in the splendid blues

of their Marine Corps, wowing all the teachers.
We recalled the Australian boy who comprehended
nothing much, till his mother, called in to help,
was heard talking fluently with him in a baby talk
they had never abandoned. They were off a farm
deeper in the mountains. A bit like the Georgian

who sat in the back of his class for one whole year
getting no English, substituting his fists for it
till he was a State champ. Unlike the Hong Kong boy who
returned to class with a slim briefcase and pinstripe
having successfully saved a million of family
investments in court before lunch time recess.

They rise up from then, Widow and Camel Driver,
now forty-fives and fifties, whom the teacher
taught to prepare and cook their halal pilaff;
they break-danced for her after midday prayers
and spoke of a friend sniped with an ack-ack gun
who vanished in red spray at his brother's shoulder.

It was a time of teenagers coaxed to go
back to such boulevards. And of helicopters
But!But!But! that sent boys scrambling
into their chair tunnels.
                    And we drove on down
at just the speed which made our tyres buzz
like the small wheels of a bed that would divide us.

High Speed Trap Space

Speeding home from town
in rainy dark. For the narrowness
of main roads then, we were hurtling.
A lorry on our tail, bouncing, lit our mirrors,
twinned strawberries kept our lights down

and our highway lane was walled
in froth-barked trees. Nowhere to swerve –
but out between trunks stepped an animal,
big neck, muzzle and horns, calmly gazing
at the play of speed on counter-speed.

Its front hooves up, planted on the asphalt
and our little room raced on to a beheading
or else to be swallowed by the truck's high bow.
No dive down off my seat would get me low
enough to escape the crane-swing of that head

and its imminence of butchery and glass.
But it was gone.
The monster jaw must have recoiled
in one gulp to give me my survival.
My brain was still full of the blubber lip,

the dribbling cud. In all but reality
the bomb stroke had still happened.

Ghost glass and blurts of rain still showered
out of my face at the man
whose straining grip had had

to refuse all swerving.

Diabetica

A man coughs like a box
and turns on yellow light
to follow his bladder

out over the gunwale
of his bed. He yawns upright
trying not to dot the floor

with little advance pees.
The clock on the night-stand
biting off an hour he hates.

Sugar, the sick caterer
managed with unzipping needles
Blood syrup, shortener of legs,

ichor of the bishop
whose name is on a school
because he could not beget.

Like many milk-blind scholars
and farmers short of breath
above billions in sweet graves.

The Privacy of Typewriters

I am an old book troglodyte
one who composes on paper
and types up the result
as many times as need be.

The computer scares me
its crashes and codes
its links with spies and gunshot
its text that looks pre-published.

I fear a carriage
that doesn't move or ding,
no inky marching hammers
leaping up and subsiding.

I trust the spoor of botch,
whiteouts where thought deepened,
wise freedom from Spell Check,
sheets to sell the National Library.

I fear the lore
of that baleful misstruck key
that fills a whiskered screen
with a writhe of child pornography

and the doors booting open
and the cops handcuffing me,
to a gristlier video culture
coralline in an ever colder sea.

All of Half Way

i.m. Sue Ridley

As I was going to Coleraine
a man in Bewleys said to me
I wouldn't wear that green cap up there
if I was you, and I snatched it off –

colours aren't yet mortal in Australia.
It was only our equestrian team cap
that you had given me, but I took
the warning, folded, to Coleraine.

There I found hospitality
and Bushmills and the Giant's Causeway.
No bush near the Mills
but a coracle sea and the Giant's columns

massing on out, a basalt grandstand
of rain-cup pillars, crimped like Rubiks
from cooling out of their rock floor
all of half way from America.

Big Rabbit at the Verandah

Big rabbit at the verandah
fleecy-chested and fawn
nibbling clover, Easter rabbit
not much like the humble

face-scratched hordes we would shoot
clear-shack! pea-shack! with rifles,
leave straining, boil for the pigs
or let stink, underground mutton

in days when yellow cows
would crop to our house doors
because undermined pasture was collapsing
seawards. We buried toothed traps

because it was war and we were losing.
Only with the cushion-udder Holsteins
our land was hard put to support
did science send our enemy

to tremble blind on dung-stony hills
Even dairy children
eased off shooting those for sport.
Grown sons restless to dress modern

compared town wages with Dad's will
and came back as grasses were healing.
Our old brindle war sickened new
settlers. Cow peas stopped being grown

and dogs gentled four-wheel-drive cattle
in through wire gates. Dairy roofs
dried to blood. After snuffed billions
Rabbit, you look edible and risen.

Being Spared the Inquests

A toddler's scream –
the bared leap of a dingo,
the boy's father running
with shouts and shovel blade.

Our valley came this close
to a deadly later fame.

Time Twins

A youth, rusty haired
as I was in my time,
rocked atop a high stool
as he read a book from
the stock he was to sell.

His left leg kinked under
his right knee, as mine does.
We had likely both of us
floated that way before birth
in separate times and wombs.

The Plaster Eater

Back to hospital again,
on the meals list, on the drip,
in for yet another stay
over an artificial knee
put in to replace a
born bone sideways wobbler.

Nurtured by mother cow
I have no idea how
a clunky knee can stop
your breath in pure pain,
unstring you as with a nerve-chop,
millions have jumped at prostheses:

a week, and they hip-hop
delightedly. Even you had six
weeks' cure, before return of agony.
Since then will have cost us a year.
Just after you were born
Europe and her limestone cities

swirled with last-breath calcium
blasted into the air
yet you tell of chewing plaster
out of your nursery wall
and how at your
first refugee-child Christmas

you ignored the candled sweets
and gnawed the pine tree's base
of calcareous brittle.
No wonder I became a teacher!
But after five children, I'm
perhaps chalk just down so far.

I, butter boy, sipper of vinegar,
am amazed as ever how you,
dear pardoner, kindest wife,
always blame yourself
as now, beyond hospital staph
and the overworking knife.

The Glory and Decline of Bread

Sliced bread (sic)
a centimetre thick
staling on forty surfaces
fit for soggy sandwiches
real bread excels all this:

high top, Vienna, cob
baguettes three times daily
breads poignant as a sob
Jewish rye and German
brothers from the hob

Tall grass waving gluten
foreshadowed cultivation
its unbloody skin-oil scent
displaced the hunting tent
for prayer and work in season –

Rice eaters do not yet disdain
all meals centering on one grain
but potatoes came, and pasta
and boi meat from old Masta
and bread put butter on the heart

the idle svelte would dine apart
once designer chefs had risen
bread turns to landfill on the shelf
or, like salt, gets smuggled in
to sit below itself.

Eating from the Dictionary

Plucked chook we called Poultry, or Fowl,
a meat rare in our kitchens, crepe-skinned
for festivity or medicine.

As Chooks alive, they were placid
donors of eggs and mild music.
Perches and dark gave them sleep.

Then came the false immigration
of millions crying in tin hell-ships
warmed all night by shit-haloed bulbs,

the coarsest species, re-named Chicken,
were fresh meat for mouths too long corned.
Valleys south of ours deigned to farm them.

When our few silver-pencilled Wyandottes
went down with a mystery plague,
their heads trailing back on their wings

no vet could diagnose them.
Chickens don't live long enough
to get sick, laughed battery keepers.

Much later, when all our birds were dead
a boy of eleven who kept
name breeds said they had suffered

spinal worm. And was there a cure?
Sure. Garlic in their drinking water.
He named a small ration per year.

His parents vouched for him. No need.
We'd seen his small flock, and the trust
that tottered round him on zinc feet.

O.K. Primavera Lips

The coral tree grows
in cowyards and old sties.
Thorny, tan in winter
it bears scarlet bracts,
red lipstick crescents.

Of Earth's most spoken word,
okay, just one suggested origin
is neither cheesy nor far-fetched:
Only Kissing. From saucy times.
Only kissing, Pa. O.K.?

In fertile soil
coral trees pout lips
all over, before greening.
Ours didn't, until drugged
with superphosphate. Now
it grips itself with carmine nails

to the heights of wisteria
that cascades rain-mauve
down wonga vines and gum trees
and the Chinese tallow boughs
ticketed with new green.

Order of Perception: West Kimberley

Water like a shambles of milk
at the end of the Wet

crowding down an ironstone flume
in the continent's roared walls

Two pinholes in England
shine their name on two lands

this one has inverted boab trees
flowering on plateaux

and water aerating its atoms
in the ocean's pumped comb

The Mussel Bowl

Of adventures by palate
lately, my finest was a soup
in which mussels had been served
and, the shellfish being shared,
no one minded my lifting up
the bowl to play
a whispered in-continuo of sup
in that yacht club down the Melbourne bay.

Growth

One who'd been my friendly Gran
was now mostly barred from me,
accomplishing her hard death
on that strange farm miles away.

My mother was nursing her
so we couldn't be at home.
Dad had to stay out there, milking,
appearing sometimes, with his people,
all waiting for the past.

Hiding from the grief
this day, I dropped off a verandah
and started walking

barefoot through the paddocks
until the gravel road
gave me my home direction.

Cool dust of evening,
dark moved in from the road edges
and the sky trees, pencilling
across the pale ahead.

Bare house lights slowly passed
far out beside me.
No car lights. No petrol.
It was the peak of war

but no one had taught me fear
of ghosts or burnout streaks
from the stars above my walking.

Canter, though, gathered behind
and came level. The rider
pulled me aloft by the wrist
Now where are you off?

Back, where a priest had just been
cursed out of the morphine room,
I was hugged and laughed over
for the miles I'd covered.

Years later, it would come down
to me that Grannie's death had
been hidden away, as cancer

still was then, a guilt in women.
One man was punched for asking
Did Emily have a growth?

A Denizen

The octopus is dead
who lived in Wylies Baths
below the circus balustrade
and the chocked sea tiles.

Old legerdemain of eight
died of too much chlorine
applied to purify the amenities
of urine and algal slippage.

Favourite of chivvying children
the one who could conform
its elastics with any current
or hang from its cupped feet

now lies, slop biltong,
beak and extinct pasta
out in the throwaway tide
and will leave with the wobbegong.

Radiant Pleats, Mulgoa

Rectangular mansion, sunburnt pink,
embracing its half-round portico
of radiant pleats, all revival Greek,
skirt or soldier's kilt: who'd know?

At least the house still stands, from back
when fellow statelies used to ring
the slopes of Sydney, issuing smoke,
watching for ships that brought everything.

Most such palaces died of equality
or of prone soldiers tucked in white.
Scant call for film backgrounds killed others
and a few were razed for spite –

Rectangular mansion, road-gang red,
tall behind its half mushroom
of swooped wood rafters, fanning to fit
the pillared curve of their bow rim.

Bird Signatures

Tiny spinnakers
of blue wrens wag among waves
of uncut lawn grass
     O
Dapper lyre bird:
wonder what he's typing there
below the study
     O
A shrike thrush whistling
so piercingly it unseats the
ballast of our mind
     O
Old river port, flooded
to mush, with bottles pacing
in it as avocets
     O
Wood sawn by Nippon,
Oz nail pulled out for a cry:
the Nankeen night heron

Last World Before the Stars

These days that we're apart
are like standing on Pluto,
there in the no-time of thought,

bijou world the area of West Australia
contra-rotating farthest out
with its three moons and little mountains,

looking off the short horizon,
the Sun a white daystar of squinch
glazing the ground like frozen twilight,

no life, no company, no nearness,
never a memory or a joke,
no pinned placket of dearness

just months gone in afternoon sleep
and cripple-hikes with beeping monitors.

1960 Brought the Electric

Old lampblack corners
and kero-drugged spiders
turn vivid and momentary
in the new yellow glare
that has reached us at last

a lifetime after stoves
put aside the iron pans
in which the skinned koala,
pelican and echidna
were laid on the coals.

How long Grandmother still
had to study whether boxwood
or mahogany baked longer
or hotter or better,
all that axed splinter cookery.

Now ah! the snapped dazzle
in the eyes of whatever
has fallen on the bed
and the wood cabinet streaming
ice cream and saltless meats.

Vertigo

Last time I fell in a shower-room
I bled like a tumbril dandy
and the hotel longed to be rid of me.
Taken to the town clinic, I
described how I tripped on a steel
rim and found my head in the wardrobe.
Scalp-sewn and knotted and flagged
I thanked the Frau Doktor and fled,
wishing the grab-bar of age might
be bolted to all civilisation
and thinking of Rome's eighth hill
heaped up out of broken amphorae.

When, any time after sixty,
or any time before, you stumble
over two stairs and club your forehead
among rake or hoe, brick or fuel-tin,
that's time to call the purveyor
of steel pipe and indoor railings
and soon you'll be gasping up landings
having left your balance in the car
from which please God you'll never see
the launchway of tyres off a brink.
Later comes the sunny day when
street detail gets whitened to mauve

and people hurry you, or wait, quiet.

Holland's Nadir

Men around a submarine
moored in Sydney Harbour
close to the end of wartime

showed us below, down into
their oily mesh-lit gangway
of bunks atop machines.

In from the country, we
weren't to know our shillings
bought them cigars and thread

for what remained of Holland's Glory:
uniforms, odd rescued aircraft
and a clutch of undersea boats

patrolling from Fremantle. The men's
country was still captive, their great
Indies had seen them ousted,

their slaves from centuries back
were still black, and their Queen
was in English exile.

The only ripostes still open
to them were torpedoes
and their throaty half-

American-sounding language.
Speaking a luckier one
we set off home then. Home

and all that word would mean
in the age of rebirthing nations
which would be my time.

Dog Skills

From his high seat, an owner
of cattle has sent dogs
to work a mob of Angus.

They hit the gravel running
and draft as ordered.
In the old milking days

dogs were apt to be
untrained mixed-breed biters
screamed at from the house

since cows had farmers
imprisoned, unable to go
anywhere, including field days

where expertise and the laconic
style were fostered. Where
whistling reshaped fingers

and words were one syll.
Now new breeds and skill
silence the paddocks

a murmured vowel
brings collie and kelpie flying
along the road-cutting

till each makes its leap
of judgement into the tractor
tray, loose-tongued and smiling front.

Raising an Only Child

Dad, this is none of your business!
You never had sisters or brothers
to fight. And you stand abashed

again, an only child. Lone species
from two multi-sibling parents
who found you a mystery.

You can be made an only child
by rivals who fail early
and give back your lullaby.

You can see sibling taught
by the instant rally of a cohort
that, were you theirs, would defend you

though with the same giggles
about bossiness or dalliance –
You do have brains, but no sense!

Expecting rejection, you tell
stories of yourself to the hills,
confused by your few instincts.

Employable only solo or top,
making friends from your own kind
is relief with blades in it,

assorted long adolescences
with whoop and giddy wit:
You can't have anything!

and *I, the only true human.*
But also reproach from your own:
Dad, you laughed and joked way more

with your rat-pack adopted children
than with us. And you stammer
I wasn't answerable for them –

Unable to flirt
or credit most advances
you sit and mourn
links of your self-raising chain.

Clan-Sized Night Chanting

Best sleeps hitching through
desert country were always
just out beyond dust-throw
of the road, deep enough in
grass to block rare headlights.

As you burnt one spinifex
tussock to make camp by
you'd hear just your blood,
yet when you'd slept a short tilt
of the Galaxy, there'd be chanting

of intersex timbre, off somewhere.
No glow of fire, though,
in any direction.
They had to be aware of you
but never shifted volume

or came to check you out.
And you felt no fear
only shyness at the notion,
as the long lines rose
parading diminuendo down.

Bread Again

The staff of life
has become
the lunch of staff

Bench Seats

Two women, a mother in black trouser suit,
polished loafers and a neck-stream of chain,
daughter in black jacket, ironed jeans,
polished loafers and a neck-stream of chain.
The sun sits beside them, way west up the Harbour.

On my own seat, a facing girl the age
of the daughter opposite is trying to strike up
conversation with the pair. Her speech has the
slight honk of a Downs syndrome accent
and the sun dazzles her, from up the Harbour.

That's. My favourite kinda jacket. I like
the crosses you got on. Too. Flat mirror metal
insignia that resemble glass.
No response is directed to her, but a whispered
grimace of mirth is shared between the women.

More from the lone girl gets scrutiny, not politeness
and suddenly both women exit to the corridor
where sunlight drives between buildings and their knees.
Who am I to moralise? Perhaps they have no English.
Only three other passengers face up-harbour,

One reads the paper, one dozes against the sun.
Only when both elegant women return
to their seats does their sidelong focus reveal
at my shoulder the man whose hiss recalled them,
and the Downs girl wears the remnants of an expression.

Grooming with Nail Clippers

After barefoot, grump and gomp
the toenail clipper is echoing
itself in the wood floor, trimming
impact ridges off outer nails.

The oblique rudder lever mis-thumbed
against its chisel opposite
crimps awry, gets re-occluded
biting corners off middle dabs.

Splitch! The entire plier skimming
under the sofa – up-heave sofa
to recover crossed arms askew
and redeploy to crop some more,

embracing your knees in opposition
you show inner thigh, and lift
toe-horn turrets which will grit
the flooring with grey beetle bix.

The Thirties

We didn't see much Depression
cutting bread and mutton to feed
men earning their family dole by tramping
the roads to find work and not breed.

Two local roads three miles apart
cockies spent three years joining up
with crowbars and shovels. Eight
other miles were hoof-churned to slop

by bullock teams, and no one could pass.
The monster logs stuck in their way
so the council gravelled the surface
and the beasts' hooves bled, grinding away

and lorries drove out into the timber
up creek beds, climbing over black stone
and the teams fetched billets for loading.
None of the cutters joined a union

or talked freedom. *Independent*, was the word
with all but the queer plainclothes fellow
who never grasped the work, and got
fat envelopes in dark Government yellow.

Bollywood Video

Us, perching on sewn vinyl bums
in the Raj, at our tables, as
more of us come bearing curries.
The wall video is tireless with drums

as its chorus-line train
stretches in along the station,
storming brakes under strain
purging cumulus of elation.

All doors undog, and troupes alight
rocking like gold-scales, as if weighing
saffron with plump humid hands
and there's the head throb, in whiskers,

boiled shirt and the undulant wail
of teen-voiced senior women.

Savoury

Brown gravy, brown gravy
should be sold by the bottle;
drink savoury, not sickly,
let your clothes catch the dottle.

Up to the Greek Club

Clung! and the shivery ascensor
climbs to the restaurant floor
and we, family, take a window table
above vast swelling park trees.
Fifty-five years I've been coming here.

This was my escape, through cuisine,
from corned beef and widower's cooking.
Of a thousand Australian Greek cafes
back then, almost none served Greek food.
This, though, was tzatzikí and panórama

yet steadier than chefdom:
souvlaki was on every day
and intellect rose to it from suburbs,
making friends and moves, till Clung!
the lift sank under vogue and aspiration.

This room, now sea-cave blue, flickered
with bow-tie waiters shouting the serves:
mia taramasalata! avoglémono!
some of us got by on oil and bread
and I never took the white ship to Athens:

Not in Zorba's time, nor Farandouri's.
Strong ethos from ancient times abashed me.
Double-breasted paratroop-shooters
I now see are all gone.
Of two senior dramatists, one hugs me.

The family and I enjoy pods of octopods
and other mezedes, and lamb and Persia's
best conquest of Greece, true rice pudding,
and we chat on over coffee hits, hearing
odd metaphors rev on the torrid street below.

Self and Dream Self

Routines of decaying time
fade, and your waking life
gets laborious as science.

You huddle in, becoming
the deathless younger self
who will survive your dreams
and vanish in surviving.

Dream brings on its story
at the pace of drift
in twilight, sunless colour,

its settings are believed,
a library of wood shingles,
plain mythic furniture

vivid drone of talk,
yet few loves return:
trysts seem unkeepable.

Urgencies from your time
join with the browner suits
walking those arcades with you
but then you are apart,

aghast, beside the numberless
defiling down steep fence
into an imminence –

as in the ancient burrow
you, small enough to see yourself,
survive crucial episodes
till you are cancelled

and a re-start of tense
summons your waking size
out through shreds of story.

Beasts of the City

Pioneers
shot their dinners and their fears
gentry were red in stag and boar
shooting hippo for the roar
turning tall giraffe to rissoles
shredding buffalo with missiles
but as true wilderness prey ran down
the hunt went sour, and in town
people talked rarity and compassion

as wild things grew rare, they urbanised
humans tardily realised:
possums quit the bush unaided
but charismatic fauna were still traded
tigers de-sinewed or Whipsnaded
orangs and howlers got sold with their forests
infective flying foxes bred like tourists
and golf course antelope and kangaroo
fattened the crocodile they drew

children, abandoning outdoors for towers,
spent glassed-in hours
combatting monstrous intestine
jag-toothed of maw and spine
while factory protein spiced with clones
grew beef or mutton, milk or bones
and the founts of these grazed free lifelong
lawnmowing, and drinking the billabong.

Whale Sounding

Enormous whale
vertically diving,
thick roof tail
spilling salt rain
off onto wallowing
upthrust all around,
bubba dog down.

The Genghis Firmament

Suspended archery of night
keeps a resplendent distance
slowly circling the Earth.

Just odd long spittle
streaks from dark iron jaws.

The Massacre

The high school echoes with gunshot,
with deadly interviews held beside chairs
by black-coated boys who will not
survive their own vengeance, despite odd
releases. You never bad-mouthed us,
man. So run for it!
                    As the cops arrive
afraid to go in, and parents
who scream to go in, a celibate
victim of years ago divines
We're shooting back now.

The Care

Carers are fifteen years younger
than you. They stop in for your boy,
they shower your mother not looking,
they unpeg and bring in the laundry.

Carers have learned the bad-smelling
jobs, and soak them as they chat.
Brown pivot stains shame a veteran –
Old age is eventually a cat

which starts on the brain of its prey
so the words come with a delay
and finally hardly at all.
Children, years younger again,

always knew the nuance of the words,
the scratchy pants, and the Latin.
Grown ups twist as the modern
approaches down gravel, down the flight-plan,

the airy and the arch,
the judgemental in starch
ampoule-filled as their hatches open.
More friends of mine now face that one

so glory to Nurse Cavell, to Nurse Kenny,
Doctor Flynn, and the sans-frontiersmen:
I brace for my turn of white cotton
and my headstone POET SO FAR then.

High Foliage

Leaves absorbing light
steep it in syrups down
into the buried world.
Leaves of a forest
feasting on the Sun.

Mind assembling below
in a language of levels
strung through soil, roots, grit,
chemistries being messaged
across moist fungi web.

Foliage is loose flight
around the top of orders:
a branch to wither,
a giant fig to fruit,
flowering to be started.

Greenest in blue and red
leaves tread on the sky
lending light its flavours
as the blind computer plays
between core and star.

The Walk-Off in Newtown

Wallow locates wallow
in black juicy nostrils
and two water buffalo
unite leisurely strolls

down a middle carriageway
dizzy with wheel-footed
wonderment and traffic-blare.
The pair advance accoutred

in grand menorah horns
tangling and clicking;
plastic tropics draggle after
the bad ad they'd been making

and people who know them
to be harmless straggle after,
reassuring the nervous,
fostering edgy laughter

in the flare of cameras
drying mud haunches
and the dignified roll
of hoof-spreading paunches

till they leave the rock track
that's been hard on knees
and fold down beside a college
under shade trees, long-grassing,

to mime a human word
of their monsoon territory –
as crews tell mirror hands
how to save the city.

Jesus Was a Healer

Jesus was a healer
never turned a patient down

never charged coin or conversion
started off with dust and spittle

then re-tuned lives to pattern
simply by his attention

often surprised himself a little
by his unbounded ability

Jesus was a healer
reattached his captor's ear

opened senses, unjammed cripples
sent pigs to drown delirium

cured a shy tug at his hem
learned to transmit resurrection

could have stood more Thank You
for God's sake, which was his own

Jesus was a healer
keep this quiet, he would mutter

to his learners. Copy me
and they did to a degree

still depicted on church walls
cure without treatment or rehearsals.

The Flute

Black night jittered sallow
blue along the south horizon
and rippled in our windows
an eerie silence in motion.

An hour, and trees in spasm
of wind as daybreak grew
pelted each other with wreckage.
Stark rain whitened beyond

the near hills, then inside them.
A whole gale bombed straight down;
except indoors, it cancelled
all the geography to vapour

and a roar like tumbling furniture
and the rain crashed off eaves.
The TV blacked and nibbled
mini coloured tape inside people

but outage didn't happen.
By midmorning in sun
and sweated flywire the garden
was re-brimming pond and cloud-lift

and the clear core of the rain gauge
drawn out, overspilled its
metrics like a champagne flute
raised to the season.

The Murders of Women

One woman a week
dies at the hands
of her husband or Other.
One woman a week
by violence in our culture.

The messageless holiday
that draws a dog's nose
in among civilian armies
and taps TV's billions
from the talk of senior women,

to the wigless divorce
not even needed now
and the children dumped on parents,
the charges screamed one night
or thousands. The one spill

after which a suit burned
or the gashes of headlights
through the car at speed –
How suddenly change came,
how often a half accident.

It brings the blue sergeants
to push down a head
still full of a war
that will feed guess-writers.
One woman. Fifty-two women.

Under the Lube Oil

Science now conclusively proves
that the skeleton under Leicester's
sainted car park was Richard III.
Being a Ricardian suits me.

If Tudor had gone bootless home
his son the queen-killer might have
worn out his galligaskins in Wales
and England remained Catholic.

The year we wintered on Culloden
legend gave us a king of our own
from five centuries earlier, also
buried under a petrol station

halfway down the Inverness road.
His name was Duncan
slain in battle by Macbeth
not in Princess Gruoch's guest bed.

Ah William, you marvel of spin.

Winter Garden

Pigeon whirr
pigeon zoom
walking the upper
khaki parterre
picking up windfall
sticks to hurl
down gully for flood
to sog and swirl away
sticks to lodge high
limbs to fall back
wirraway crack!
pigeon zoom
grass pheasant whirr

Goths in Leipzig

Black was pouring out
of the Kaiser's mighty station,
kohl mingling with floral:
it was the Goths, dressed not prole
but precarian, crossing
sunken tramway of the Platz
in balmoral and crinoline
besoming the pavement up
into the city's Kultur precinct,
Goths of half Europe,
clad in gilet and swart ruff
leading small chimney children,
bolero and culottes and
gold-buttoned mariachi pants,
nothing military or uniform,
chest hair T-shirted in voile
strolling in the rung clangour
of Sankt Nikolai post Mass,
Goths, parading not marching
a funereal insouciance,
older tourists silencing qualms
at any European unison.

Maryanne Bugg

What woman wouldn't camp out, in trousers
for a man pinched and bearded as the nine
lions on the courthouse coat of arms
with their tongues saying languish and lavish?
In winter, he was Fred who worked down
the Manning for Murrays, but come warm days
he was Thunderbolt on high New England
who took her from slouching white men
and white women's dreadful eyes.

The New England future highway was formed
by Christian men who reckoned
Adam and Eve should have been
sodomized for the curse of work
they brought on humankind
but roads were game reserves to Thunderbolt
when a bridge was a leap on a horse
and wheels laboured, trundling thru splashways.
Tell Fred I need to be robbed Friday
or I'm jiggered! The game was half slapstick.

That German band that Thunderbolt
attended by a pregnant boy,
bailed up on Goonoo Goonoo:
Gentlemen, if you are that poor
I'll refund your twenty pound, provided
a horse I mean to shake wins at Tenterfield.
And it did, arching its neck, and he did
by postal note at Warwick.
Hoch! Public relations by trombone.

Acknowledgements

Poems in this collection have been published in the *Adelaide Review*, *Archipelago*, the *Australian Book Review*, the *Australian Poetry Journal*, *Chimera*, *Commonweal*, *Entanglements* (Isle of Lewis), *First Things*, *4W Magazine*, *Hermes*, *Little Star*, *Magma*, *Melbourne Review*, the *Monthly*, the *New York Review Gallery*, *Notes for Translators*, the *Paris Review*, *Poetry Chicago*, *PN Review*, *Qualm*, *Quadrant*, *Rialto*, the *Reader*, *Subtropics*, the *Spectator* and the *Times Literary Supplement*.